The Ongoing Life and Times
of the
Almost famous

PHYLLIS FISHER
(Tall Tales and True of a Legendary Past)

Rainey Leigh Seraphine
Wizzenhill Publishing

Copyright© 2020 Rainey Leigh Seraphine
Wizzenhill Publishing

All rights reserved. Without limiting the rights under copyright reserved above, no part of this work/publication may be reproduced, stored in or introduced into a retrieval system, or transmitted, in any form or by any means (electronic, mechanical, print, photocopying, recording or otherwise) without the prior written permission of the copyright owner.

ISBN   978-0-6487768-1-9

Dedicated to Phyllis' children,
Brian, Rodney, Joy and Michael,
their children and the generations who follow.

I sincerely thank Rodney for inspiring me to write this,
it has been an honour and a pleasure.

Above all, I thank you Phyllis
for your time sharing memories
and inspiring me with your stoicism
to become a better person.

I also wish to thank Helen Hannah for her support of this project and the valuable information I was able to extract from her book: "Together In This Jungle Scrub ... A Folk History of The Comboyne Plateau"

INTRODUCTION

In the souls of our elders, stories lay sleeping and the late 1890s saw Comboyne Plateau become home to the spirits of some wondrous stories.

In their determination, pioneers settled and shaped the village and surrounding lands, turning a remote, isolated, rainforest covered mountain into a thriving community.

Comboyne's heyday, through the mid 1900s had 120 dairy farms, several schools, cafes, a butcher, hairdresser, banks, supply store, baker, blacksmith and more.

Roughly 100 years later, Comboyne has fourteen dairy farms, one public school, a rural store, one cafe, one small supermarket, a post office, a petrol station and the Comboyne Club. Why this decline? Perhaps the arousal of those sleeping stories will shed some light.

We start with the story of a woman, born in the late summer of 1927. Her family moved from Herons Creek to Toms Creek, at the base of the Comboyne Plateau. She was nine years old.

Some 80 years later, Phyllis Fisher is a well known and much loved character, in fact, her renown spreads far. My first impression of her is a soft, humble woman with an acute mind as her memory recall is astounding. She still spends most hours in her lush, two acre garden tending her plants, peacocks and guinea fowl. Saturdays see her at the local tennis court, honing her skills.

She is a delight to meet and her stories are an inspiration. Understandably, they are not told in a strict lineal sequence. As with all recollections, the most memorable tend to permeate through past and present with a will of their own.

I hope to do justice to her family in the recording of these stories for all who follow, and I am grateful to have Rodney and Michael, two of Phyllis' children sit with us as they infuse their mothers' recall with their own childhood perspectives, growing up on the family's dairy farm.

Geographically, The Comboyne Plateau is 56 kilometres west of Port Macquarie on the mid north coast of New South Wales. The Plateau is a volcanic plug with its peak rising to 700 metres. At the time of settlement, only one rough hewn track had been forged from the eastern side of the mountain via Kendall. The first settlers arrived by boat from the coastal village of Laurieton, south of Port Macquarie.

Herons Creek is inland from Port Macquarie on the highway and Toms Creek sits a few miles below the western side of the Comboyne Plateau.

Chapter 1 - Girlhood

As a young girl, Phyllis Flanagan had no interest in playing with dolls or stitching embroidery. An adventurous spirit led her outside where flora and fauna whispered their secrets and Phyllis followed their call. Her father worked for the Herons Creek Mill, driving the bullock teams hauling logs.

"I wanted to go to the mill with him, but he wouldn't let me. He took my older brother instead and I could never understand why. Although, now I can imagine what a nuisance a little girl would have been in the bush.

I've always loved birds and when I was about four, I wanted to fly like they did. Outside the shed where Dad fed the bullocks was a huge tree stump. I thought it a good height to learn to fly. So I climbed up onto that stump and leapt off, flapping my wings. Of course, I crashed and didn't try again."

When Phyllis turned five, she joined her older brother and sister on the walk to Herons Creek school, half a mile from home.

Her brother Charles, nicknamed Bardy for some reason she doesn't recall, was given a push bike for Christmas and he started dinking the young Phyllis on his new wheels.

"He had the handles turned up and I used to sit on the bar in the middle. I had a little suitcase with my

lunch in it. Like most young fellas, he was inclined to speed. He called it 'moting', but I think he made that up, I don't think it was a real word. This day we were flying, or moting as he would say, down the dirt road when my suitcase got caught and both of us, including the bike, somersaulted over a gutter in the road. My elbows and knees were badly skinned and he refused to take me after that."

Industry was progressing. Tractors began replacing bullock teams and the Herons Creek Mill wished to modernise its operations, but Phyllis' father had no interest in machinery. Against his mothers' wishes, he moved the family to Toms Creek, an area three miles down from the top of the Comboyne Plateau. It was Easter 1936 and dairying was on his mind!

Unpredictable weather challenges most aspirations and after replacing his bullock team with dairy cows, not a drop of rain fell for the next six months, in spite of the areas well known rainfall. The cows died, forcing him to find work elsewhere.

He had uncles living on Comboyne and helped clear their land in his younger years, so the terrain was familiar and work was plentiful for strong men felling the Comboyne scrub. He eventually acquired around forty dairy cows. Phyllis remembers it well.

"Our first milking machine was called an MDK: Mum, Dad and the Kids! Us kids weren't very big at that stage, but we still had to help. So we'd milk in the morning then do correspondence school when lessons

arrived by mail from Sydney. As soon as our lessons were finished, we'd race out to the paddocks and have the rest of the day off. I hated it when a school opened in 1938, I preferred being home with the cows."

Phyllis soon learned that a proficient dairy farmer could milk around nine cows an hour. She remembers sitting on wooden blocks instead of the traditional three legged stools.

"I think that's cause of my Irish grandfather, who lived at Herons Creek. He was a hot tempered old fella. They had a few cows too and when a cow kicked him, he'd pick up the stool and ram it into her ribs breaking the legs off the stool. In compassion for the cows, they gave him heavy wooden blocks to sit on, ones he couldn't lift so easily. I guess Dad followed the same tradition!"

Phyllis discovered cows could be just as hot tempered.

"If you had a grumpy cow, you'd have to tie her leg with a rope which has a loop in the end. It goes around the cows leg and you slip the other end through, tying it to a bolt. She can't kick and spill the milk when she's tied. It sure hurts when they kick.

I've still got my fathers old leg rope hanging in the shed, the one he used when he grew old and only had one house cow."

In spite of 180 square kilometres of rich, red basalt soil and perennial creeks, farming was treacherous with the steep terrain and the luxury of quad bikes for herding cows was unknown. Even if they had been invented, the early farmers of Comboyne were not affluent and with isolation and lack of roads such luxury would have been a distant dream.

Dogs were used to bring the cows for milking. Phyllis remembers a particular incident which some may find disturbing. Wastage was not tolerated and a frugal lifestyle with common sense saw them do what they had to for survival.

"It was steep where we were, not really dairy country at all and the dog brought the cows in for milking. One morning, this old cow called Lucky was trotting down the hill when she stumbled and broke her neck. She was a good cow with a good gallon of milk and not wanting to waste it, Dad grabbed his bucket and milked her anyway. He would always say: 'you can't waste a drop of good milk!'

Of course, there was no veterinary service this side of Kempsey, so unless you could fix animals yourself, you had to shoot them. The carcasses would be dragged away for the dingoes. It was pretty primitive when you think about it."

Forty years after first settlement, roads were non-existent in spite of government promises. By the time Phyllis' family arrived in the area, tenacious settlers had solved some of the problems themselves as teams of men forged much needed roads with picks and shovels, using heavy hammers to break the larger rocks. This created a spidery network of dirt roads around the plateau, making it easier for farmers to access the goods and services of the Comboyne village.

The Butter Factory had been in operation since 1914 with designated depots along the ridges of the Plateau. The farmers would deliver their cream to the respective depot for pick up by the cream lorry which was just a horse and cart. The Flanagans had their depot on the top of Ducks Ridge.

Pack horses were used to transport cream to the depots. The pack saddle front strap went around the horses chest with the back strap going under the crupper, or tail. Four metal hooks would fit over like a saddle. The Comboyne blacksmith made short chains with a hook on each end and the cream cans would hang on the hooks, one on each side of the horse. Most cans held eight to ten gallons, but the Flanagan horses couldn't carry that weight up steep hills so they filled theirs to six gallons.

When Phyllis was fourteen, it became her responsibility to get the milk to the depot as her brother had enlisted in World War II and was sent to Papua New Guinea. There were five girls in the family by then and they had to take over his work on the farm.

"You'd lead the pack horse up the hill until you reached the dirt track. Then you'd 'drive' it, riding behind on another horse. It would take at least an hour to get to the depot at the top and you'd hope someone was there to help lift the cream cans off the horse. They

were heavy.

The cream lorry brought clean cans from the factory. Any supplies we had ordered were put in the cans. They'd be hung on the horse and carted back down the hill."

I cannot imagine a fourteen year old girl taking on such a regular task, yet Phyllis doesn't describe her childhood in terms of hardship. The work had to be done so she did it. Her acceptance of such responsibility at a young age is stoic and inspiring.

"It wasn't much fun when it was raining though. Especially when the saddle got wet after getting off the horse to open the gates. There were seven gates and two sets of rails between home and the depot, so I'd have a really wet behind by the end of it."

I realise I am stating the obvious here, but it seems necessary to truly get a feel for a seemingly innocuous job! Seven gates and two sets of rails meant getting off the horse, opening the gate, driving the two horses through, stopping to shut the gate, get back on the horse and do it all again at the next gate or rail. Of course, that was just on the way up to the depot, she had to come down again too. Cream was taken to the depot three times a week in summer and twice a week in winter and Phyllis did it in torrential rain, freezing cold or extreme heat. I will no longer grumble at getting in and out of my car for one gate, even in pouring rain!

Making butter was also an arduous process. With nothing but a wooden spoon, it would take two hours of stirring before the creamy goodness was ready for spreading, but if the cream was warm, it would take longer. Ingenious solutions made life a little easier if creeks were handy to homesteads, as the women kept their cream cans in the cold creek water before churning.

"We made butter by hand until we discovered you could buy a butter churn. We ordered one and it came to our depot in a crate. The churner was heavy with a cast iron base which you'd put on a slab of wood and bolt down. It had a big metal bowl and flat paddle with cogs attached to the handle. You turned the paddle around in the cream until it turned to butter.

We had this old grey horse called Trip, because she was always stumbling. When I had picked up the new butter churn from the depot, Trip and I were coming down a particularly steep part of the hill and the crate must have been digging into her ribs. She didn't like it and started to buck. She bucked that crate and the cream cans right off and I had to crawl down the cliff face to pick everything up. Then I had to catch the horse again.

The metal part of the churn didn't break, but the bowl had a big dint. Dad had to beat it out with a hammer of course, but it always had a dint. I did that job until my eldest brother came home from the war and Dad retired."

With the help of butter churns, the whole process only took 20 to 30 minutes, depending on the thickness of the cream. It must have seemed like heaven compared to two hours of monotonous arm exercise!

The cows would sometimes graze on different types of weeds and Phyllis describes it as giving the butter an awful weedy flavour. At that time, it was only the cream sold to the factory and the skimmed milk was given to the animals and used for cooking. Cooking with the goodness of whole milk was considered wasteful.

The milk was kept in the dairy where it was covered with gauze for ventilation and mesh to protect the cans from the summer blow flies, until it was time to take it to the depot.

Separation of milk from cream was done by hand with a bowl holding roughly six gallons. It had a tap, spouts and a float which would regulate the milk so it didn't overflow. The cream would come out at the top and the skimmed milk would stay in the bottom.

Phyllis remembers when they started dairying.

"Butter was six pence a pound, that was how much the farmers were paid. But then, you could buy a penny ice cream when I was a kid too, if there was any available. We didn't have refrigerators."

Milking was a family chore with all hands on deck and children had to participate before and after school. As the plateau's outlying farming community grew, more schools were built making travel distances shorter. With precious little spare time during the week, game shooting on weekends was a popular pastime for the boys. Pigeons, bush turkeys and wallabies were plentiful and in fact, the early settlers supplemented their dinner tables with the local fauna. Charlie, Phyllis' brother, also enjoyed shooting.

"When he was about 15, my brother went shooting one afternoon. Standing on a steep hill he saw a wallaby further down and took a shot. He knew he'd injured it but the wallaby bounded off. Charlie bolted down after it, jumped over a gully and broke his ankle.

He was lying in the paddock about a quarter of a mile from the dairy and I was walking with my younger sister, Enid. Apparently she'd been playing up, and Mum and Dad made me take her for a walk. I could hear my brother screaming, so we ran back to tell our parents.

Dad thought Charlie had shot himself of course, and took off. On finding him with a broken ankle, he ran to the neighbours farm where two old bachelors lived and got one of them to help put a splint on Charlie's leg.

It was 8 o'clock at night by the time they had everything ready. They put him on a stretcher and the two of them dragged him up the hill, cutting a track in the dark as they went. He was a sturdy kind of fella my brother, so it wouldn't have been easy.

Of course, there were no telephones and it was about three mile over a big hill between two farms and over the other side to our Uncle Tom's house. My great uncle, Tom Duck was the only man around who had a car. I suppose he was sitting relaxing in his house when they arrived. He drove them to Wauchope hospital where the doctor set his ankle and put it up on a pillow. It slipped off the pillow during the night and broke again. After that, he had a limp and a bent ankle all his life."

When the original settlers to Comboyne arrived by boat in Laurieton, a coastal town south of Port Macquarie, a dirt road was cut from the village of Kendall and Lorne, a few miles inland. It wound its way up the eastern side of the Comboyne mountain. To this day, some 115 years later, it is still a dirt road, *sporadically* maintained by the local council.

Apart from the pot holes and corrugations, it's a beautiful thirty minute drive by car from Kendall, especially when the sun or mist is filtering through the trees. It would have taken much longer by horse or bullock, hauling families and their belongings up the mountain. Phyllis remembers the story of one family.

"One of the early settlers brought his bullock dray, furniture and the family altogether. They were coming up through Lorne and when they got to where Swans nursery now is, discovered it was too steep for the bullocks to pull the load. Thinking they'd come back, they chucked all the furniture on the side of the road. But they never did go back for it and made a makeshift

table with a few slabs of wood, used butter boxes as seats and it was years before they could afford real furniture. That's a typical farmer!"

In spite of the work and time involved with dairying, families were close and visits with relatives were important. The Flanagan family rode horses down to Herons Creek to see Phyllis' grandparents.

"It was just a track from Toms Creek to Herons Creek and we had to ride through the river as there was no bridge. It took about six hours and that was really trotting along.

Dad and I used to drive cattle from Herons Creek too. My grandparents had property and we got a few old jerseys and heifers from them, to keep us going. It would take around three days to drive them back to Toms Creek.

When I was going to school, Dad was working on the road and ploughed a lot of cuttings with a team of twelve bullocks. There wasn't much money around, this would have been in 1940. I liked working with bullocks and when I was thirteen I'd get up early, have something to eat, catch the horse and ride with Dad to the bullocks, which were kept on a neighbours property. We'd muster them into the corner where the fence was L shaped and I helped yoke the team up. Then I'd ride to a neighbours house, have a proper breakfast, get dressed and go to school. That was five days a week. I could yoke a draught horse or a team of bullocks when I *was 13 and I still can!"*

I was stunned. Phyllis is now an 89 year old woman of slight stature and to me, a team of bullocks is a formidable sight, yet she can still yoke them. I can't help but picture her peers sitting comfortably on couches, weaving their magic via needle and thread as Phyllis works with her massive bullocks in the dust or mud.

As with work stories, it's a delight to hear family tales of precious time spent together when the days chores were over.

"Dad had two sturdy male bullocks, one called Tiger and one called Jersey. These two bulls used to fight when they weren't yoked, I guess they were figuring their pecking order! When Dad came home from work my sister Enid, I think she was around two, would be crawling around the kitchen floor growling at Dad: 'I'm Tiger and you're Jersey'. Dad would get down on his hands and knees and they'd pretend to fight on the kitchen floor. From then on, Enid was nicknamed Tiger. She's now eighty and even my adult children still call her Auntie Tiger."

I asked Phyllis about an old story of a blizzard in Comboyne around 1942. She would have been 15 at the time.

"We were living at Toms Creek and this day Dad had taken the cream up to the depot. Our creek, which

was just down from the house had flooded and us kids were barefoot, having a great time floating paper boats down the swirling water. When Dad came down to fetch us, he told us it was snowing on Comboyne and the cattle were freezing to death. I heard later that the frozen cows were standing against the fence and once thawed, they all fell down dead! A lot were lost that day."

Of course, climate wasn't the only cause of drastic change for the early settlers. In 1941, structured education came to an abrupt end for Phyllis.

"I left school at fourteen because my mother was having another baby. I had to stay home and help my older sister look after the kids and milk the cows. Mum was away in hospital for about a month, so I had to leave school. That was the end of my education."

I asked her about the old schoolhouse on the Boorganna side of Comboyne which was moved to Toms Creek. Phyllis told me about the new teacher from the city who had been appointed. A horse was acquired for his transportation but he'd never ridden before.

"When we first saw him jerking and bouncing up and down on his horse, we couldn't help laughing at this new teacher. Of course, us kids were accomplished riders so it looked hysterical seeing an adult ride like that. But he was nice and on really hot days, he would take us all down to the creek where we could dangle our

bare feet in the cool water while he read us stories."

It's a picturesque scene, far removed from city school life.

Country kids can be resilient, some walking many miles to school barefoot. Not all families could afford shoes at various times. Quite a few aged Comboynians told me about walking to school this way and in winter, they found welcome relief for their frosty feet by standing in warm, fresh cow manure. It is truly innovative, as only kids can be and it seems none were the worse for such practises.

I'm reminded of these stories as we are bombarded with advertising on the dangers of germs. From cockroach and flea bombs to fly and insect poisons, we now have chemicals and antibacterials to protect from the horrors of nature. We can awash our lives with 99.9 percent surety but I wonder about the 0.1 percent which survive!

The Comboyne community continues to grow and for all their hardship and isolation, life also demands rest, relaxation and entertainment. Gatherings at neighbouring farms were common where experiences and concerns could be shared and eased. Many a tired and weary heart would be lifted with stories, music and food. Sometimes a gathering continued until early the next morning when breakfast would be shared before guests headed home to milk their cows. Visits also served to make sure neighbours hadn't suffered disaster. Early settlers sometimes arrived to find a neighbour had died, so with no phones and miles between farms, the bush telegraph was a slow system.

Welcome relief from stresses and hard work was also provided by the Comboyne Hall where The Nite Lites, a popular band performed. Someone usually had a liquor license and sold bottles of beer. Phyllis said the men drank outside behind the hall.

"It was civilised drinking back then. Dad used to come with us when we were 15 or so but once we were a bit older, he said we had enough sense to go on our own. So we used to ride up from Toms Creek and tie the horses to the trees in the Uniting Church yard. If you left them out on the street, the young fellows would let them go or put your saddle on back to front or do something else silly. Some of the boys around Comboyne were real larrikins.

There was a dressing room in the back of the hall and we'd change into our good clothes then dance all night and ride home around 2 o'clock in the morning.

In the hall, chairs were placed against the walls and the band was down the end. Us girls would sit on the chairs and the boys congregated outside the hall until they had the courage to ask us to dance.

Some boys who lived down the Lansdowne Road would come, but they were too shy to ask girls to dance. Their father would say: why don't you ask them? But the boys would answer: what if they say no? So they'd stand at the door staring in at the dancers and when they got home their Dad would ask: how'd you go tonight boys? And they'd say: not a bloody dance!

Of course, the popular girls would be danced off their feet and the plain ones would sit like wallflowers. It was a funny sort of situation, the town boys would only dance with the town girls and the boys from farms would dance with the farm girls; some kind of pecking order I suppose. I think the town boys felt themselves a little better than the farm boys. They probably thought: 'oh yeah, well you have manure on your feet' and I guess there was some truth in that!"

When she was 16, Phyllis remembers going to a New Years Eve dance with her sister Mary, who was 19. The dance was held at Ellenborough, quite some miles away but torrential rain had been falling on the mountain and of course, they would have to go on horseback. Naturally, their father didn't think it a good idea as the river at Ellenborough was in flood. But with two headstrong teenage girls, he gave up. They rode off and managed to get down to Ellenborough, wet but unscathed and tied their horses. As with most halls, the room at the back was used by girls to change into their good clothes. Phyllis didn't say what the dance was like, I think perhaps the following story took precedence in her memory, but around midnight they decided it was time to head home.

"I'd sometimes nod off a bit on the ride home but the rain was torrential and of course, it was pitch black; although I guess there must have been some patches of moonlight. We managed to get through the Ellenborough River but I had to lift my feet out of the stirrups 'cause the water level was so high. I was glad we had left when we did! We got across okay and the horses stopped at the next set of rails. There was a gully on the other side and the water had become a raging torrent. Both our horses started to snort and buck 'cause they didn't want to go through it. I thought there must be a good reason so I let my horse go around the top end where it wasn't so deep. But Mary just yelled 'git up' and her horse suddenly bolted forward and plunged into the swirling water. She and the horse completely disappeared out of sight."

Phyllis laughs as she remembers. By now, her sons Rodney and Michael have joined us and are quietly listening to this story about their mother and aunty when they suddenly burst into laughter.

"Yep! I'll bet that shocked her," said Michael.

"Well, it wouldn't have been very pleasant," laughs Rodney, "all that water would have gone under her raincoat and straight up her skirt."

"In from the bottom and in from the top," drawls Michael.

"Imagine sitting in that for another two hours on the ride home," muses Rodney, "squelching away on a wet saddle..."

Phyllis gets back to her story.

"They all but disappeared. Then suddenly re-appeared on the other side of the bank with great gushes of water streaming down. I've never seen anything like it.

My best dress was really stained with the dye from my coat 'cause we didn't bother changing when we left the hall.

I guess we're lucky the horses knew their way home in the dark too!

Mary's horse, Old Don used to be a racehorse before we bought him. One time we were coming home from town and turned off the road onto Ducks Ridge where there's a flat, straight bit. We started to canter but old Don got the bit between his teeth and he took off, racing down that straight flat to the boards. When he got to the bend, he was going so fast his legs started plaiting and he barely turned the corner. I thought he was going to somersault. Mary's just hanging on yelling at him: git up then if ya wanna go, go on ... and he did!"

Apart from communal dances and neighbourly visits, listening to the wireless also provided relaxation, entertainment and news gathering.

"We had a gramophone and then about 1938 we bought our first Breville wireless, a big ugly looking thing powered by a six volt battery.

We had to take the battery on the pack horse to the depot so it could be sent to the butter factory for charging. Of course we had two batteries so we could still use the wireless while the other battery was getting charged. But you still had to restrict what you listened to, it would run flat pretty quickly. You couldn't just turn it on every morning. It was a real menace having to pack that thing, six volt batteries were really heavy. You'd put it in a corn bag, hang it on one of the hooks of the pack saddle and then balance with a bag of rocks or a can of cream so the saddle wouldn't slip. We did that for years!

We listened to Martins Corner, the old Dad and Dave show and at midday there was a country and western show for half an hour from 2TM Tamworth and we listened to the news, especially during the War."

Memories are precious, especially where animals are concerned. Living on Comboyne, I often see large herds of black and white fresians peacefully grazing in a paddock. It's a serene vista I love and to me, they look like one entity. But I had heard they each have their own personality and I asked Phyllis about it. She has a few stories which she wonders might shock me.

"My father was a bit inclined to think he could educate animals with his shotgun. Old Moth was a cunning cow. When she heard the dogs barking and saw you riding up the hill, she'd go and hide. So we put a bell on her. But when she saw us coming, she'd sneak into the bushes knowing the bell wouldn't ring if she stayed really still.

Dad was getting the cows one afternoon and noticed Moth's backside sticking out from the bushes. He had his shotgun over his shoulder and got back about 50 yards or so and fired at her behind. Of course, it peppered her with the shot and she came charging out of the bushes, straight for the dairy. After that, all you had to do was clap your hands and yell: c'mon Moth, and she'd come a running."

Who can deny a bit of shotgun education? It worked in this case and the cow was none the worse for it. Michael explains they are just like people.

"Some are sneaky old bastards and each one has a different personality. Rodney has two hundred cows and the first one out of the gate will always be one of two or three cows and there's always the same laggers. You know which ones are hiding in the bushes too! They may move in a mob, but they're all different."

There is another story about Trip, the stumbling horse, but as I am not a farmer, Michael has hand drawn a picture of a horse with a sled attached so I can understand the scene.

"Trip was the pack horse and my father had this brainwave to break her into wearing low traces so she could pull a sled. Usually the draught horse pulled the sled but it wasn't always easy to catch him, unless you had a bag of chaff and he was really big. We had an old sulky collar suitable for Trip and the traces to drag a sled. The chains go from the collar through the back band and hook onto the sled. The traces, or chains go past the horses fetlock.

So we got her in the cow yard where the dairy was and yoked her up. Dad got hold of the reins and yelled: git up Trip! As he turned her around, the trace chain came up against her back leg and she let out a screech and started to buck and kick. I had never heard a horse screech like that before. She kicked frantically with both back legs as she galloped around the yard. My father was holding onto the reins yelling: whoa Trip, whoa old girl.

In the process, the sled started falling to pieces. She was kicking the boards apart and the timber was flying past Dads ears. She literally kicked it to pieces and when he eventually got her settled, there was nothing left of the sled. She had been racing around the yard with just the two trace chains hanging down. It would have gone on around five or six minutes, this kicking and screaming and carrying on and him saying 'whoa Trip, whoa Trip'. But she didn't take any notice, she was petrified. It would have made a good scene in a movie.

We didn't know that Trip had smashed up a sulky before we bought her. Something had really frightened her and anything that touched her back legs would send her flying.

I used to have to carry a stock whip to drive her up to the depot with the cream. When you were behind her, she'd look round at you with one warning eyeball. If you were too close, she'd lash out and kick you in the shins and it really hurts. Of course, we weren't told of this trait when we bought her."

Horses can suffer 'Queensland itch' in hot weather. Their sweat causes severe itching and they'll firmly rub the butt of their tail or neck on anything solid. Phyllis remembers Punch, their old draught horse.

"We had an outside toilet up the hill, about thirty or forty yards from the house. Of course, they were all outside in those days. It was a small weatherboard shed with a pan toilet bolted to a block of cement and it sat on the bank of a gully which was mostly dry until a big rain. Punch used it as a scratching post.

One day Dad went to use the toilet, but it was gone! Punch must have had a really itchy backside as he stood up against the back of the toilet shed. He would have been moving backward and forward, backward and forward until he dislodged the shed off the cement block altogether and it rolled down the bank and landed in the gully. So Dad got to work with some timber. Of course, there was always plenty of timber around. He made a new floor and stood the toilet up exactly where it had landed in the flat of the gully, after rolling down the hill. That's where it still stands today."

Rodney and Michael marvel at how well the outhouse must have been built to not fall apart.

"The toilet shed wasn't the only spot Punch used to ease his itching. Dad had made a big wooden gate with a high pole on the hinge side and another pole formed a triangle above the gate. This stopped it dragging on the ground when you opened or shut it.

Punch used to get his head through this triangle gap and scratch his neck, going backwards and forwards, backwards and forwards, as usual. He constantly knocked the gate off its hinges. Dad got a bit sick of this. One morning, he saw Punch at it again, so he went up the hill with his shotgun. He fired a shot into Punch's behind and when the pellets hit him, he let out a great snort and plunged ahead taking the gate completely off its hinges. He bolted down the paddock towards the creek with the whole gate hanging from his neck. Dad had to go down and rescue him and the gate. But it never stopped Punch doing it.

He was a funny horse, originally from Broken Hill. He was frightened of running water because he grew up on a farm which only had bores and troughs. We couldn't get him to cross the creek. He'd snort and buck and you literally had to drag him through. It was a long time before he got used to it. He was a quiet old horse too. A funny old thing."

"Quiet until he got his arse shot!" adds Michael. "He did a lot of work in his day, did old Punch."

Bush felling and burning was a regular occurrence on the plateau. The scrub was felled with axes to make new pastures. When the timber had dried, it was burnt to clear the area for sowing seed. One such burning got out of control and the fire took out the fence and bridge between the neighbours, just below their bullock pen.

"When they lit that fire it was 115 degrees in the shade at Toms Creek. So Dad decided to put a new bridge in. He still had his bullock team from Toms Creek, so he cut a great big log which needed to be dragged up to Apple Tree ridge, across the crown and down to the gully so the bridge could be made.

But the bullocks were having a bad day and wouldn't pull it. Dad got a bit frustrated. He had his whip and said to me: 'now Philly, I'll cut you a myrtle stick and when I stand the bullocks up, you get along the offside and lay into them.' So he got along the near side with his whip and when they stood up and the chains began to tighten, I got my whippy stick and started laying into them, from the tailers to the leaders. I'm lashing into these bullocks and they slowly started pulling, which proves they were really just being lazy. Once they got it going, they kept going and I was able to stop. I looked around and one of the neighbours was standing there, laughing his head off! He thought it was the best thing he'd ever seen. The bullocks dragged the log up to the ridge and then down to the gully and Dad made the bridge. It's still there I suppose."

Phyllis recalls an incident with her Uncle Marty. He had wanted to enlist when the war started, but in a bid to convince him to stay, his mother gave him 100 pounds so he could select a piece of land on Toms Creek. He agreed and started dairying. He purchased a bull from old Mr Carey down at Killabakh, a small village on the road to Wingham.

"He had a Hereford stud farm and Uncle Marty bought a young bull from him. Mr Carey told him that when a bull or heifer charges and goes to horn you, they shut their eyes just before they hit you. Whether this is true or not, I don't know. But old Mr Carey said if you're standing there and they start to charge, the minute before he hits you with his horns he'll shut his eyes and you can knock him down with a big stick. 'But you gotta be quick Marty,' he said.

Anyway, Uncle Marty had this nasty heifer down at the farm and he said to Dad: 'You let her out of the yard and wait till she charges me. I'll knock her down as soon as she shuts her eyes. That'll teach her.'

So Dad let the heifer out of the yard and she charged straight down the hill towards Uncle Marty. The next thing, Uncle Marty's flat on his back on the ground and the heifer is charging off down the hill. He wasn't quick enough."

"Ya gotta be quick Marty," Rodney and Michael chorus, laughing.

Phyllis says it's been a family saying ever since. Any situation that requires a level of urgency starts with 'ya gotta be quick Marty'. But it seems Uncle Marty was a bit slow. I wondered if the heifer was incredibly fast.

"She was very fast," say Phyllis and Michael in unison.

"Or she forgot to shut her eyes," laughs Rodney.

CHAPTER 2 – THE COMING OF AGE

Girls were taught knitting, sewing and crocheting; spending their nights by kerosene lamps stitching for their glory boxes. Phyllis, being a nature lover, bullock yoker and pack horse driver didn't show much interest.

"I remember when I was 18, people would ask me what I had in my glory box and they were really shocked when I told them: 'nothing'.

Oh that's terrible they'd say. Oh dear, you gotta have a glory box. What if you want to get married?

These girls had doilies and runners and all sorts of tablecloths and fancy works. Eventually, I must have been bullied into it I suppose. I started making a few doilies and crocheting around the edges but I was never really into it. I'm an outside person and was always climbing trees and collecting birds eggs. I remember Dad telling me I shouldn't take the eggs away from the poor little birds. But I always figured they could lay more. After all, they've got nothing else to do!"

I imagined marriage prospects on Comboyne were rather slim, but Phyllis said most farms had workers from on and off the mountain so there were many boys around.

"My father usually had a working man of some description on the farm and that's where I met Hilton. I

couldn't stand the sight of him for a long time 'cause I thought he was a bit of a 'know-it-all,' but we married when I was 21 'cause getting married and starting a family was the fashion. I never thought anything strange about it."

Moving onto a share farm near her parents, Phyllis and Hilton settled into married life. As it was only a few miles from her family, she'd visit them every couple of weeks. Share farming was a common practise for people who owned property and couldn't manage on their own. Profits were shared by half, as were the costs but it was not a profitable arrangement so Hilton often worked away from home, felling scrub while Phyllis worked on the farm.

"The owner used to make hay and he had a lucerne patch. Hilton wanted to be a modern farmer and strip graze that patch, so he bought a battery operated electric fence. But it's not a good idea to strip graze lucerne. I had to really watch the cows because too much lucerne will bloat them. I'd give them ten minutes then chase them out and make sure they didn't head for the creek which was close by. If they drink with a stomach full of lucerne, they'll bloat and I was terrified of that happening. I didn't know much but I knew you could stick a knife in them and let the gas out, but you've got to know what you're doing or you'll kill them. Gas builds up and it chokes them. They explode from the inside I guess and it's not something you want to let happen. It's a painful death."

Rodney explained that sticking a knife into the hide of a cow, even when it's pumped up and bloated is extremely difficult. Using a pocket knife, you could easily close the knife on your fingers and chop them off.

"Or if you could get them into the dairy and put a tar stick down their throats, it makes them belch and get rid of the gas that way," added Phyllis. *"But I always managed to dog them out of the creek and get them up the hill before it could happen."*

Phyllis often worked on her own, even when Hilton was home. She remembers him tying a young bull to a tree and the bull becoming angry and upset. Tugging against the rope, it caught Hilton's thumb, ripping his entire nail off.

"Hilton was out of action for two or three days with his thumb bandaged. He could work with one hand, but he wouldn't do very much. He was fairly reckless and accident prone.

We had forty cows and three milking machines at that stage and an old, Ronaldson Tippet motor which drove the machines. I was milking by myself and often, this stupid machine wouldn't start. It was a coot of a thing! You had to turn it with a handle and crank it. I felt like kicking it sometimes, it was a real beast."

Hilton had grown up in Kempsey and was more of a 'town boy'. He considered Toms Creek somewhat uncivilised. They moved twice more to other share farms on Comboyne. Unlike Hilton, the owner of the last property was content and staid in his old farming methods and Hilton found it frustrating.

"He wanted to be a modern farmer with the new equipment they had now. Then this place (the house we are sitting in) *came up for sale and we've been here ever since."*

She tells me of an old saying: 'women have a baby every corn pulling'. That's once a year, but Phyllis had been married for two years before she fell pregnant with Brian. Rodney came three years later then Joy after eighteen months. Finally Michael arrived two years after Joy.

Mothers had to take their babies and young children with them to the dairy as there was no other choice. Winter meant waking them out of warm beds and carrying or walking them in the chill early hours of the morning to a cold dairy shed. It also meant keeping them safe while milking. Of course, by the time the children were older, it was their job to take care of the siblings.

"When it was just Brian, I'd put him in a wooden box when I milked. Everything came in wooden boxes those days. We used to sit this box on a 44 gallon drum and sometimes he'd stand up in the box and rock it back and forward. Occasionally he'd fall off! He was a bit of a danger.

Then when the others came, I took all of them. Brian used to walk, Rodney and Joy were in a stroller. I'd put the kids in a box so they wouldn't get mixed up in the milking. They used to scream a bit, but you'd take their dummies and bottles for them."

Milking machines were dangerous for small children to be around and I had heard about a child from Sydney who was sent to relatives on a Comboyne dairy farm. It was during the war when fears of the Japanese bombing Sydney were very real. He was kept safe from the milking machines, but the separator had a moving shaft and belt and the child had grabbed hold and was killed. Accidents can happen easily and it's almost impossible, as any parent knows, to watch children every minute. But children also create many memorable moments.

"I can remember living in the old house, when they were little. I had three of them laying side by side on the linoleum floor with their heads on pillows, sucking their bottles and all three had their feet sticking straight up in the air."

It's a touching scene. Not so touching was Rodney's childhood passion for rolling mud balls and sticking them up his nose. Of course, once the balls had hardened, Phyllis said it was really hard to get them out.

"I don't know why anybody would make little mud balls and poke them up their nose!" says Phyllis.

"Is that what happened to me nose?" laughs Rodney.

With this snippet of Rodney's history laid bare, I felt compelled to ease his embarrassment. Heroically, I launched into my story, not realising he wasn't the slightest bit embarrassed! My own younger brother did the same when he was around two. He used gravel from our driveway and the small pieces of carrot Mum painstakingly diced for snacks. I vividly remember her laying him on the kitchen bench and shining the torch up his nose for the extraction process. I thought my brother was one in a million. Cheers Rodney!

But Phyllis says her children never caused her much concern. They didn't really go anywhere to get into trouble. They used to run around the paddocks and their father put them to work on the farm when they were young, helping to milk and muster the cows. Brian drove the tractor when he was around twelve years old.

"Kids driving tractors on steep terrain is pretty dangerous, but Brian managed okay. He had a rally car too when he was older. He was always a mad driver!"

When he was old enough, Brian went to University. He wasn't interested in farming. For Rodney, the farm was his passion and like his mother, hated school. To his teachers disappointment, he left at 15.

"The teacher wanted him to go to college and have an education so he could become an accountant. He said Rodney was a mathematical genius and it was a

waste him being a dairy farmer."

Both Rodney and Michael laugh at this and I can't help chuckling a little too. We all know Rodney is a farmer to the core, it's in his blood.

Hilton often worked away from the farm, building many of the houses on Comboyne, the Comboyne Club and working on the local co-operative.

"He always wanted his own property, but he never wanted to settle down or be a farmer. He'd bring in extra money though."

So Rodney took over the farm full time in 1960. His father as overseer, made the decisions and paid the bills. Phyllis helped Rodney with the milking but Michael wasn't happy to work at home and left at the age of 15.

"He went down to Bundanoon and got a job on a Hereford stud but it didn't work very well. They made him live in a tin shed and he had to wash in the creek so it was pretty feral. It taught him a bit of a lesson though, he didn't think home was so bad after that. He came back and found a job with another dairy. Then he worked in the milk factory in Comboyne for years, driving the milk trucks to the railway at Wingham. Now he has his own stud farm. Joy went to teachers college. Rodney is the only one who stayed home to work on the farm. The others have come and gone."

Other memories are flying and Michael has us in hysterics as he vividly recalls an incident with Gulliver, the draught horse. Phyllis yearned for a tennis court and after some initial preparations by Hilton, he went away to work again leaving Michael and Rodney to finish the job.

"The old girl had a whim," tells Michael, *"she wanted a tennis court. So the old fella, in his usual manner, built a fence up around the top side and down the back, but he never finished it."*

"As usual," interrupts Phyllis.

"We built this triangle shape with boards bolted together and a ring on the end to drag it with chains. A load of clay was delivered by 'Shoob', one of the locals, which needed to be levelled, hence the triangle. So we harnessed the old draught horse, Gulliver who was a bit flighty. The old man, in his wisdom, always had a draught horse regardless of whether we needed one or not. Gulliver was only used once in a blue moon, so of course you can imagine he was round and fat as a fool and fresh as buggery."

Rodney adds to the story.

"I used to keep my dog chained on a long wire between his kennel and the chook house and the dog used to go back and forward along the wire."

"Anyway," continues Michael, *"Mum and I harnessed Gulliver and I was sitting on the back corner of the wooden triangle, holding the reins. But I cut a corner too sharp and the triangle ran up Gulliver's heels. He didn't like it and took off in a frenzy as I rolled off the triangle with my legs up in the air. Gulliver bolted between the gate posts and the triangle got jammed, snapping the chain off as he headed straight to where Rodney had his dog tied up in the kennel. But the swingle bar was still attached and it and the horse went round and through and over the top of the dogs wire. It tore the wire down and next I saw them all disappearing over the embankment at 80 miles an hour. The horse, swingle bar, kennel and dog, all going in a big ball over the bank."*

"Off the ground!" recalls Rodney, *"yep, they were bouncin' away. The dog came loose about fifty yards away while the horse went to the bales at 80 mile an hour. When we caught up with him he was standing in the corner of the bales,"* adds Rodney.

Phyllis is laughing as she tells of poor Gulliver going round and round in the cow yard snorting and careering.

"Hilton went off his head," adds Phyllis, *"he yelled that we'd ruined the horse and didn't have any sense. Of course, he wasn't here as usual."*

"I can still see the dog and the kennel," laughs Rodney, *"they were flying six or eight feet off the ground*

at one stage."

I asked Michael if he'd been hurt.

"Nah, I just rolled off all innocent. I got up okay but my eyes were probably popping out watching the whole scene. I still get a chuckle about the dog. I couldn't believe Gulliver just picked him up, the kennel, everything and took off."

Phyllis thinks it would have been another great movie moment and Rodney swears:

"Me dog was never the same since. But that dog knew never to chase the horse!"

CHAPTER 3 - THE MAKING OF GIRRAWEEN GARDENS ... AND SCONES!

Phyllis helped Rodney milk for years and when she retired from farm work, her love of gardening took precedence. The two acres of paradisical garden are proof of her creativity and ability with iridescent turquoise peacocks, a magnificent pair of white peacocks and guinea fowl roaming between natives, exotic plants, magnolia trees, orchids and a plethora of other flowering shrubs and trees. Stonework, a large fish pond, hand made waterfall and meandering walkways were, and still are her backdrop and passion.

Brian had the idea of a pine plantation for income. They ordered 1000 trees, a mixture of Radiata, Taeder and Slash pines. When the bare rooted saplings arrived however, many of them had died and those that survived were stressed. Hilton promptly rang the company and they sent another 1000 pines.

The kids helped plant this massive amount of saplings. At the time, Phyllis and Rodney recall getting water to them 'a bit of a problem'.

To this day, I love driving past those tall pines and peering in through the forest. Sometimes you see Rodney's cattle in amongst the trunks. The pine needles often cover the road and there's something about this pine forest which soothes the soul.

The peacocks still roam the dirt road outside her driveway with their magnificent display of courting tail feathers and mystical bird call. It's breathtaking as you approach. Unfortunately, the white pair eventually succumbed to the growing traffic. Every time I saw them, I thought of Spanish brides in white and many a turquoise tail feather has been 'souvenired' from the roadside.

Port Macquarie is a destination for overseas tourists after they arrive in Sydney. The Ellenborough Falls, at Elands via Comboyne boasts the second largest single drop in the southern hemisphere and attracts innumerable tourists.

The guest book at a local cafe, the Udder Cow shows comments and signatures from interstate and overseas visitors who went on to visit Girraween Gardens and Ellenborough Falls.

Hence, Girraween Gardens, as the family home is called, became well known too and visitors would enjoy Phyllis' Devonshire teas and walk around her magnificent gardens.

The official tourist information sign displaying "Girraween Gardens...6K" still stands in the centre of the Comboyne village, confirming Phyllis' unintentional tourism success, but it's more affectionately known by us locals as Mrs Fisher's garden. I ask her how it became so famous.

"A bus driver from Port Macquarie used to take tourists to Ellenborough Falls. He had a mini bus for seating half a dozen or so tourists. On his way back one day, his radiator boiled out the front here and he came in asking for water. He said I had a nice garden and asked if I would consider doing Devonshire teas for his passengers on a weekly basis. He said it was hard to keep them entertained and a stop for tea and scones in

my garden would be good for them."

It was a smart plan, as the drive from Port Macquarie to Ellenborough Falls would be almost two hours each way in a minibus on a dirt winding road. Phyllis had never considered tourism and wasn't used to dealing with the general public, but the thought nagged at her.

"I went to the tourist bureau and asked them what they thought. They warned not to put too much money into it as it might never get off the ground.

So I bought a few cups, plates and containers and learned to bake scones. I thought I'd be doing the bus one day, then they'd be gone for a week. But people heard about these tours and came separate to the buses. I'd be gardening away and they'd just turn up any old day. I had to put a time on the gate in the end because I've had them sitting in the garden at 8 o'clock at night in the summer, playing guitar and singing. And coming here at sunrise begging for Devonshire tea. That's how it happened, when the buses started to come."

I asked Phyllis what her kids thought of all this and Rodney piped up, "*bloody Devonshires.*"

"Yep, bloody Devonshires," adds Michael.

"Bloody Devonshires," laughs Phyllis. *"I'd be doing teas when they wanted me to do something else for them."*

By this stage, Brian had become Director of the Bureau of Agriculture and Economics in Canberra and two of his work friends turned up in Phyllis' garden, unannounced. As usual, she was outside working after deciding to clean out the fish pond. Up to her elbows in green slime and muck, she was acutely embarrassed at them finding her in such a filthy state!

I was interested to find out what was on the property when she and Hilton first bought it, especially around the garden. She told me there was no garden, just the old farm house and an unexpected intruder.

"The house had been empty for 12 months when we came to look at the property. A couple rented it for 18 years and when they retired to Port Macquarie, sold the dairy herd. But one cow was probably up in the bush somewhere at the time and missed being part of the sale. Being a bit of a rogue, she'd ended up at the house and pushed the front door open and we found her in the end bedroom. It couldn't have been for too long, because she was okay. We bought the house and there was a lot of cleaning to do, especially in that bedroom!"

Many years later, Phyllis and Hilton built a new house on the property, but the old one is still standing, surrounded by a magnificent bamboo plantation.

Phyllis kept working on her garden. She remembers when she decided to build a waterfall down an embankment below the old house.

"This was in the early 1950s when the two McMillan boys were around 17 and 18. They were standing up on the bank with their hands on their hips, looking down at me. One said to the other: 'I believe she's making a garden down there. That woman must be bloody well mad.'

Eventually when I had started Devonshire teas and I was making a bit of pocket money, they said: 'you know, we thought she was mad when she started making that garden, but look at it now.'

Time went on and the buses kept coming. One bus driver suggested Phyllis enter her garden in the Sydney Morning Herald Garden Competition. She knew nothing about competitions but they eventually talked her into it.

"I'd never been in any competition in my life so I didn't know what to expect and they don't let you know when they are coming. One day, Michael and I were busy doing a bit of paving near the wishing well and we'd created a huge mess. A car stopped out the front and a man got out and walked up to us saying he was the Sydney Morning Herald garden judge. I looked around at the state of the unfinished paving and thought 'oh dear'. He commented on the mess, so I took him for a walk around the whole garden. I was in the North Coast zone of the competition and I won first prize with a certificate and a plaque.

Then others from the Hastings Gazette came and asked me to show them around too. I told them about the McMillans calling me a bloody madwoman and all this came out in the paper the next week and I nearly had a fit. I didn't know they had used a tape recorder.

I won the North Coast Zone right to the Queensland border. I've now got prizes hanging up in the old house, a few silver vases and all sorts of things which I guess need polishing.

I almost got famous. I don't know that I wanted to be famous."

Memories from Phyllis' Sister, Colleen

Our brother, Alwyn relayed a story last year which I vaguely remembered, but I was only a small child at the time. He would have been at school so I think it was in the early 50s. Those years were extremely wet and a huge landslip came down in the back paddock and Punch managed to get himself bogged up to the neck. Sometimes I wonder if he had a death wish! Alwyn went home to get help but had to wait until Bardy had finished milking. Bardy had taken over the dairy when he married.

They harnessed the other two draft horses and went to the rescue with ropes and chains. It would have been half a mile away. Punch was bogged too deep to put the chain around his body, so they had to hook it around his neck. When they pulled him out of the bog, Alwyn said his neck had stretched about two feet. It's just as well Punch had a very thick neck! They dragged him onto a grassy patch and released the chains, giving him a gentle kick in the ribs. He struggled to his feet and wandered off to live a few more years. I remember Punch as a very old horse with a grey muzzle so he must have lived to a considerable age.

Regarding Phyllis' story, I think she had a fairly tough life as a young wife, not uncommon for farm women of that era. Dairying and caring for four young children was no picnic, especially when Hilton was working away. Just as well she was used to roughing it.

At one stage she was working in a dairy at Boorganna, quite a few miles away, yet living where she is now so she rode a horse to work.

I think her garden became an outlet and recreation away from hard farm work. Our mother was a talented gardener too and although not on the same scale as Phyllis, she grew beautiful roses and always had a superb vegetable garden. Actually most of us enjoy gardening, with varying degrees of success. Our mother also won prizes for flower arrangements in later life when she had more time! Maybe it's in the genes.

I also remember the old toilet. Dad called it the 'toilo'. Eventually Hilton put a little addition onto the back verandah and installed a septic toilet but Dad wouldn't use it. He'd say: 'I'm not using that toilet' and every morning, he'd walk out the gate and up the gully to the toilo.

A note from the Author

I had interviewed Phyllis and her family when I was still living on the Comboyne Plateau and at that stage, I knew nothing about self publishing, so this story stayed in file format on a USB stick.

Three years ago in 2017 I moved to the Coffs Harbour hinterland and discovered the joys of self publishing. I found the USB stick tucked away in a drawer and yearned to have Phyllis' story published so her memories wouldn't be forgotten and her descendants could learn their heritage.

Phyllis is now 93 and resides in a nursing home. I confess I can't imagine her not pottering around her two acres of paradisical garden, but I suspect her stoicism and love of the outdoors, including her ability to work hard most of her life has helped her to live to such a beautiful age.

You are an amazing woman Phyllis and I feel much gratitude for having a part in sharing your story.

With love,
Rainey

www.ingramcontent.com/pod-product-compliance
Lightning Source LLC
Chambersburg PA
CBHW041500010526
44107CB00044B/1519